Exploring Careers in the
CREATIVE ARTS

Don Nardo

ReferencePoint
Press®

© 2024 ReferencePoint Press, Inc.
Printed in the United States

For more information, contact:
ReferencePoint Press, Inc.
PO Box 27779
San Diego, CA 92198
www.ReferencePointPress.com

LIBRARY OF CONGRESS CATALOGING-IN-PUBLICATION DATA

Names: Nardo, Don, 1947- author.
Title: Exploring careers in the creative arts / by Don Nardo.
Description: San Diego, CA : ReferencePoint Press, [2024] | Includes
    bibliographical references and index.
Identifiers: LCCN 2022061217 (print) | LCCN 2022061218 (ebook) | ISBN
    9781678205683 (library binding) | ISBN 9781678205690 (ebook)
Subjects: LCSH: Creative ability--Juvenile literature. | Art--Vocational
    guidance--Juvenile literature. | Professions--Juvenile literature.
Classification: LCC BF408 .N3447 2024 (print) | LCC BF408 (ebook) | DDC
    153.3/5--dc23/eng/20230222
LC record available at https://lccn.loc.gov/2022061217
LC ebook record available at https://lccn.loc.gov/2022061218

CONTENTS

Showing the World One's True Self

"When you're creative, you live differently," writer Sergey Faldin points out. "You may have to live with your parents until 30 and seek work. Maybe you'll go work at a Starbucks to pay the bills and create your masterpiece at night. Or maybe you will quit your job to pursue your calling. You'll do all sorts of weird stuff that normal people don't do."[1]

Faldin bases this description on the hard reality that creative people tend to have a difficult time building a career based on their artistic passions. This is partly because there are usually far fewer job openings in the arts than there are creative people to fill them. Also, fair or unfair, there is also a long-standing societal tradition in which the vast majority of such jobs pay relatively little. "By and large, artists have a tough time," says Jonas Almgren, director of Artfinder, a company dedicated to helping artists sell their work and make a living. "It's sad to say, but the starving artist syndrome is still very much there. It's not easy to make a career as an artist."[2]

Almgren's comments reflect information gathered by the company when it surveyed thousands of creative artists living and working in the United States and Europe. The study found that fully three-quarters of US artists make less than $10,000 a year. Close to half earn $5,000 or less annually. One of those American creatives, writer Tim Rettig, discovered how real an artists' lack of earning power can be. "You want to be an author?" he asks. "Film producer? Painter? Musician? Regardless of what your craft is, you are most likely going to struggle financially for quite a long time in the beginning of your career."[3]

No Single Reason

Despite the widely recognized difficulties of making a steady living as an artist, there is never a shortage of individuals in each new generation who vigorously and earnestly try to do so. It is only natural to wonder why that is.

There is no single answer to this question. Numerous reasons have been given over the years by fine artists, designers, craftspeople, and other creatives. Some claimed the main object of entering the arts is to achieve an emotional connection between the artist and his or her audience. The famous Russian novelist Leo Tolstoy, for instance, said, "The activity of art is based on the capacity of people to infect others with their own emotions and to be infected by the emotions of others."[4] Other creatives have said that they engage in artistic pursuits because they need to earn a living and their particular art forms are the only ways they know to make that happen.

One's Reason for Being?

These diverse assertions aside, far more often creative artists say they do what they do out of pure enjoyment. The noted early twentieth-century English writer Virginia Woolf referred to her most intrinsic motivation to create as her "rapture," saying, "Perhaps this is the strongest pleasure known to me. It is the rapture I get when in writing I seem to be discovering what belongs to what, making a scene coming right, making a character come together."[5]

Similarly, many artistic people say that they create because they cannot imagine doing anything else, as it is a necessary component of their soul or their very reason for being. In Michigan textile designer Chris Triola's words, "To be creative is the most exciting thing you can do. It's as necessary to me as eating and breathing."[6] Expanding on that idea, California painter David J. Rogers states, "From the earliest time that I can remember, I've always wanted to be an artist. I can't remember a time in my life that it wasn't my primary focus. Although my life's journey has had many twists and turns, this is the place I've always come back to."[7]

FACT
One recent study found that three-fourths of artists in the United States earn less than $10,000 a year.

Thus, a good many creative people cannot be scared away from pursuing their crafts by warnings of how little money they will likely make, because in their minds such pursuits are not a matter of choice. They have to follow their dreams in order to be emotionally or spiritually fulfilled. Faldin sums it up aptly when he tells fellow creatives, "Like any artist . . . you've got a void inside of you [and] the only thing that can fill this void [is] art. Or addiction. Because they are essentially the same thing." It is better, he says, for a creative person to embrace who he or she truly is inside. "Show the world your true self," he advises, "through your work and your art."[8]

CHAPTER ONE

Art Directors

What Are the Careers That Art Directors Pursue?

In the ranks of the world's creative individuals who work in the arts, art directors tend to be among the most multitalented and well paid. They work in a variety of career fields and have different responsibilities depending on the specific job. Some art directors, for example, supervise or work on staffs in advertising agencies, in public relations companies, on newspapers, and for book and magazine publishers. Others work for the producers and directors of movie, television, and live theater productions. And still others make their living at companies that create board games, video games, and scale models of trains, ships, cars, rockets, and so forth.

One thing all art directors have in common is that they are highly imaginative. That is, they use their talent and experience to envision, decide, or fashion the overall style of an artistic project, whether it be for a magazine, film, game, or other visual venue. Often this vision has a unifying element. This is because it may bring together the efforts of a few, or in some cases many, other creative people. In such instances, says James Fenton, founder of Blimp Creative, a design firm in Taiwan, "as an art director you must be a leader, someone who inspires and guides the vision of the design team. You have to be able to recognize the talent in those around you and learn how best to get the best from them."[9]

How Do People Prepare for Careers as Art Directors?

With occasional exceptions, the vast majority of art directors are expected to obtain a bachelor's degree in some area of art or design. Typical of such areas are graphic design, interior design, fine arts, and photography. A few would-be art directors go beyond a four-year degree and get a master of fine arts degree. Those who do so increase their chances of finding high-paying positions later.

Most prospective employers also prefer to hire art director candidates who have had at least some previous work experience in a creative field. Examples of jobs in such creative fields include illustrator, interior decorator, and web designer. In fact, a majority of aspiring art directors have four or five years of work experience in another creative occupation before becoming art directors. According to the Bureau of Labor Statistics (BLS), such work experience in creative areas "develops an art director's ability to visually communicate to a specific audience creatively and effectively."[10]

No less important than a college degree and work experience for a prospective art director is developing a suitable portfolio. For an artistically inclined person, a portfolio is a collection of work samples that demonstrate his or her creative abilities. It is an essential element in job hunting because managers, department heads, and others involved in hiring art directors expect it and will look at it, often at length.

How Well Do Art Directors' Jobs Pay?

No standard or set salary for art directors exists. Indeed, there is an exceptionally wide range of salaries possible, depending on a person's education, experience, talent; the particular nature of the job; and other factors. Tara Wasmer, an art director for a scale model company called TWH Collectibles, explains, "Art directors

can get paid anywhere from $40,000 to six figures depending on where you live and the kind of company you work for. Top ad agencies pay top dollar for good art directors. When you are in more of a niche market in a smaller city, you are likely to get paid significantly less than that."[11]

Nevertheless, every few years the BLS calculates a median salary for members of this profession. In 2021 the median annual salary was $100,890. The lowest-paid art directors—those in the smaller local markets that Wasmer mentions—earned less than $57,000 in 2021. On the other end of the scale, the highest-paid art directors earned an impressive $194,000 that year. Most of the members of that elite group worked in movies or television, while the lowest-paid art directors tended to work for newspapers and book and magazine publishers.

Choosing the Appropriate Locations for a Movie

Among the many duties of an art director for a movie (often also called a production designer) is to scout locations—places such as buildings, city streets, forests, beaches, farms, or mountain settings that are mentioned as principal settings in the film script. "I needed to find the kind of run-down, seedy areas of the city where the little con-man, Ratso, would normally hang out," said the late stage and film art director John Robert Lloyd (*Midnight Cowboy*, *John and Mary*, *The Boys in the Band*). Here, he recalled his location scouting for *Midnight Cowboy*, which won the Academy Award for Best Motion Picture in 1969. Lloyd continued:

> We used those places for exterior establishing shots, mainly. Most of the interiors were sets built on the sound stage. It would have been too difficult and expensive to get electricity into the abandoned buildings, light them, and then cart in an entire film crew and all that heavy equipment. So much simpler to just reproduce a few rooms in the studio, where you have more control.

John Robert Lloyd, interview by Don Nardo, Mount Kisco, New York, January 9, 1969.

Helpful Skills

In addition to a certain amount of education and experience, successful art directors require a set of skills that place them in a category of talent well beyond that of the average person. First, to excel at the job, an art director must have strong communication skills. This is because he or she has to be able to listen to and confer with employers, creative staff members, and sometimes clients in a clear, preferably pleasant manner. This helps minimize misunderstandings or misgivings and ensures that whatever project the company is working on will move along smoothly and meet the expectations of the clients.

An important corollary of an art director's ability to communicate with the members of his or her staff—whether they are few or many—is strong leadership skills. Not only must he or she be able to effectively engage them verbally, it is also essential to be adept at organizing them and delegating the right duties to the right people. In addition, the art director needs to have the ability to motivate his or her assistants to do their best at all times. The ability to manage time is also key for this job. The best art directors possess an inborn ability to know when enough time has been spent on a specific phase of a project and when to move on in order to keep the project on schedule and within budget.

Still another helpful skill for art directors is the ability to take criticism in a professional manner. It is quite common for them to receive criticism from their bosses and/or clients. And there is little or no room for outbursts of temper, hurt feelings, or other unprofessional behavior. As Wasmer emphasizes, "You have to have tough skin and not take criticism personally."[12]

What Are Typical Working Conditions for Art Directors?

Because art directors are usually surrounded by or at least in frequent touch with staff members, bosses, and clients, the profession is a fairly social one. Typical locations include office complexes, busy art studios, theater stages, and movie and TV sets filled with all sorts of creative people. Some art directors do design work from home, but even then they take breaks to communicate with staffers and others via phone, email, or Zoom.

A Typical Workday for an Art Director

As any art director will testify, the profession has no typical day. Indeed, every day is different, whether he or she works for a magazine, design firm, or film or television producer. Still, certain activities and duties will recur at varied intervals once or twice a week or a few times a month. For example, during a campaign or project, an art director might spend a full day or perhaps two or three full days figuring out how best to present that campaign or project overall, either in print or visual form. Then, parts of one or more other days will usually be spent determining which photos, visual designs, and other design elements to employ. The art director will likely also

FACT

According to the BLS, in 2021 the median annual salary for an art director was $100,890.

11

spend other parts of those same days developing the financial budget and timeline for the project, which might span a week or two or several months.

Once the visual look, budget, and timeline have been determined, the art director will have a sit-down with the client (or clients), a meeting that might last part of a day, a full day, or on occasion a couple of days. The client may approve the project there and then, but it is not unusual for a client to ask for one or more changes. If that occurs, the art director must spend a certain amount of time revising his or her approach to the project.

After full approval is obtained, art directors typically switch gears and begin working closely with their staff. Thereafter, they spend their days coordinating activities with assistants or entire artistic and creative departments. Over time, other staff members will show the art director their individual contributions to the overall project, and in each case the art director will either give approval or ask for revisions. If the project is for an advertising firm or a publisher, many of those working on the project will be graphic artists, writers, or editors. Or if the project is for a television or film company or Broadway show, staff members will more likely be set decorators, carpenters, lighting designers, or special-effects technicians.

Thus, an art director's workdays tend to be highly varied and complex and require him or her to be a highly creative person with innate leadership abilities. James Fenton summarizes it well, saying,

> The role of the art director could be compared to that of a chef, fusing together ingredients to produce a menu of delightful dishes. All designers [on his or her staff] inject their individual personalities, tastes and style into the work. It is the art director's role to identify and understand the different flavors each member brings to the team, and then carefully infuse them to complement one another.[13]

The Need for an Impressive Portfolio

All prospective art directors require a portfolio, a collection of samples of a creative person's work, which he or she typically shows to potential employers at job interviews. A portfolio should be as impressive as possible, as explained here by Luke O'Neill, a digital artist at THG Studios in Manchester, England.

> Whether you're a recent graduate, a seasoned pro applying for a new job, or a freelancer scouting for new work, you need a powerful portfolio. Curating [selecting the items for] and maintaining your portfolio should be an essential part of your professional life. In essence, your portfolio should showcase your professional work, demonstrating what you can do and the skills you have. But more than that, it should demonstrate your experience and the journey that you've been on to get there. Needless to say, it's no simple task. . . . Ensure that all the pieces in your portfolio 100 per cent represent your best work. If you're unsure whether or not to feature a piece then, as a rule of thumb, you probably need to ditch it. The work featured should demonstrate the very best of what you can do.

Luke O'Neill, "How to Curate a Creative Portfolio," Creative Bloq, March 1, 2019. www.creativebloq.com.

Find Out More

Art Directors Guild (ADG)
https://adg.org
The ADG provides mentorship, supervision, and on-the-job training for future art directors. The organization's attractive website showcases the talents of both practicing professionals and up-and-coming designers and artists as inspiration for young people contemplating joining the profession.

National Endowment for the Arts (NEA)
www.arts.gov
Created in 1965, the NEA is the largest funder of the arts and art education in the United States. Its website features extensive information about how artists, including designers and art directors, can obtain grants, as well as up-to-date postings about ongoing and new creative projects of various kinds.

One Club for Creativity

www.oneclub.org

One Club for Creativity (formerly the Art Directors' Club of New York City) promotes the advancement and success of creative artists, especially art directors, writers, and designers. Its website details how the organization holds an annual contest for the best young prospective art directors, designers, and other artists, with awards for the winners.

CHAPTER TWO

Craft Artists

What Are the Careers That Craft Artists Pursue?

Craft artists are highly creative people who make artistically attractive or valuable objects using their hands and selected, often specialized tools. *Craft arts* generally refers to artwork that is functional or has a specific or useful purpose—often in the home. Examples of craft arts include quilts, wooden bowls, ceramic plates, glass vases, and jewelry. Even when this artwork is displayed—in a gallery, for example—rather than used for its intended purpose, it can still be considered craft art.

Among the most familiar craft artists are potters (or ceramic artists), woodworkers, metalworkers, jewelry makers, glass artists (often called glassblowers), textile crafters, quilters, and doll makers. Each of these crafts includes specialties, many of which have come to be seen as separate crafts in their own right. In the area of woodworking, for example, some practitioners are so-called traditionalists. This is because they create traditional-style furniture, dinnerware, utensils, and other objects inspired by the works of past generations, such as those of colonial times or the nineteenth century. In contrast, some other woodworkers create new styles and are often referred to as contemporary or avant-garde woodworkers. For example, Pennsylvania-based Wharton Esherick, who died in 1970, was famous for fashioning tables, chairs, and other furniture items that featured unusual curves and odd angles.

Similarly, artisans who work with textiles, a specialty sometimes called fiber arts, might specialize in spinning, dyeing, weaving, or embroidery. Some primarily weave, others mainly embroider, while still others employ all of these processes to make fabrics for clothing, furniture coverings, wall decorations, and much more. Moreover, some textile crafters work with uncommon or unexpected fibers to make cloth. Popular San Francisco-based fiber artist Pam DeLuco, for example, often uses wax from bees and silk from silkworms to make hand-spun thread that she spins into highly specialized cloth.

Whatever a craft artist's specialty might be, she or he requires a studio or other dedicated space in which to work, create, and make a living. A majority of craft artists—roughly 60 percent, according to the Bureau of Labor Statistics (BLS)—are self-employed, working either out of a public shop or studio or from a home studio. Most of the rest work in shops or small factories owned by someone else.

How Do People Prepare for Careers as Craft Artists?

Preparation and training for craft artists can vary widely, depending on the craft itself. No specific academic schooling or other formal training is required for someone to become a craft artist. In fact, outside of a few individual courses in a small number of colleges, as a rule most colleges do not offer comprehensive degrees in such artistic areas.

FACT

According to the BLS, roughly 60 percent of craft artists are self-employed.

Far more commonly, beginning craft artists learn from other, more experienced artists. That is, those newly entering such fields tend to become, variously, apprentices, interns, or other kinds of assistants to established craftspeople. In some cases such an expert is a parent or some other relative of the younger person, and over time, knowledge of the craft passes from one generation to the next within a family.

This is the case with the Craven family of potters in North Carolina. Over more than two centuries, nine generations of Cravens have turned out distinctive, finely made examples of ceramic art.

A Self-Taught Metal Sculptor

Most successful craft artists learned much of their trade apprenticing with or otherwise assisting artists already established in a given craft. But a few were self-taught, often beginning in their teenage years. A good example is noted UK metalworking artist Anthony Tanner, best known for his busts of the Asian religious figure the Buddha. In recalling how he taught himself the trade, he refers to jackdaws (crow-like birds that are said to be drawn to shiny objects):

> I've always been a bit of a Jackdaw attracted to shiny metal—and I have always enjoyed making things, so I decided to have a go at stainless steel sculpture. . . . [I] bought a load of very ancient, very cheap [machine parts] and transformed my garage into a workshop. Then began a long and very steep learning curve. . . . I became a self-taught metal worker and metal sculptor and . . . after 6 months of hard work my first large piece emerged. . . . Family and friends were very surprised by the result which had been under wraps till completion—"you seem to have a knack," said one. . . . From then on I was hooked and it became a passion.

Quoted in Smart Artist Hub, "Life Experience, Metalwork & Buddhas: An Interview with Anthony Tanner," 2022. www.smartartisthub.com.

It all began in the mid-1700s, with the family's first potter, Peter Craven. His son, Thomas, followed in the trade, but it was Thomas's own son, the Reverend John Craven, who became the family's first truly great ceramic artist and today is considered one of the greatest early American potters. Regrettably, no examples of his once famous works survive, but art experts think that several of the surviving examples of the pots made by his son Anderson capture the father's style. Examples of Anderson's works, along with those of later generations of Cravens, are on display at the Mint Museum in Charlotte.

Many craft artists have no family members practicing their chosen craft and therefore must find other ways to learn from professionals in that field. This typically involves an apprenticeship, in which the less experienced artist works for the established artist while also learning his or her techniques. Thousands of craft artists, including potters, woodworkers, and metalworkers, have

followed such paths. Massachusetts potter Andrew Jones, for instance, recalls how he "secured low-level employment at a pottery studio, mixing clay and glazes, doing odd jobs, and all the time listening to and learning from skilled potters who taught me the basics of the craft a little at a time."[14]

How Well Do Craft Artists' Jobs Pay?

According to the BLS, the median annual wage for most craft artists was about $50,000 in May 2021. Those in the lowest-paid 10 percent made less than about $22,000, and those in the highest-paid 10 percent earned more than about $126,000. As a rule, the lowest-paid craft artists are the ones who work either part time or full time as helpers in established shops or studios.

By contrast, the highest-paid individuals in these crafts are most often the owners of such businesses, especially ones that have gained regional or national prominence.

Helpful Skills

Aside from talent and creativity in working with their chosen materials, most craft artists demonstrate many of the same basic abilities and skill sets. They tend to be adept at organizing their creative supplies and resources and in managing their work time over the course of days and weeks. Such skills are, after all, essential to constructing the finished products in successive stages. Craft artists also need to be able to visualize how such a finished product will look after being shaped from diverse, initially formless materials. In many cases, business management skills are also useful, considering that many craft artists market and sell their own creations. In addition, some crafts require the artists to have at least some abilities normally associated with carpentry and other trades. From a potter's standpoint, Jones explains, "not only do you need to be an artist, but also a carpenter, electrician, and plumber—not in the professional sense, of course, but some of the skills of those tradespeople are necessary for success in ceramics."[15]

FACT

According to the BLS, in 2021 the median annual wage for most craft artists was about $50,000.

What Are the Working Conditions for Craft Artists?

Most craft artists spend many hours working alone. In part this is because the process of creating any kind of art has traditionally been a fairly solitary activity. Another reason that craft artists frequently do much of their creating by themselves is that most of the time these crafts involve one person making single objects one at a time, with little or no need for someone else to help. Moreover, such work is typically time-consuming. Fashioning a glass vase or carving a wooden figurine, for instance,

From Whittler to Craft Artist

Although the vast majority of creative artists know from an early age that they possess certain artistic talents, a few do not discover that fact until adulthood. A notable example is well-known Welsh English wood-carver Giles Newman. After recovering from a serious illness in his late twenties, he started whittling pieces of wood to pass the time and soon found, to his surprise, that he had a natural talent for intricate wood-carving. He soon had created a number of small wooden horses, birds, and other animals. Then, he recalls,

> a friend suggested I [try] to sell them. It had never crossed my mind. Straight away, I started to build up a following, particularly in America. In the first 12 months I had 30,000 followers on Instagram and pieces sold within two minutes of going online. I was gobsmacked [shocked]. I had to pinch myself. The fact that I could pick up a piece of wood from the ground, carve it and someone would part with their hard-earned cash to buy it is still deeply humbling.

Quoted in Great British Life, "The Art of Whittling Sticks in West Lancashire," December 11, 2017. www.greatbritishlife.co.uk.

can take anywhere from a full day to two or more days. What is more, it is not unusual for such a craftsperson to suddenly decide he or she is on the wrong track and discard the first attempt and start over. As a result, most craft artists create a personal working space, or physical niche, of some kind where they can be alone to do their work in the manner they prefer. The talented Welsh English wood-carver Giles Newman, for example, says, "I've set up a shelter with a tarpaulin at the end of my garden and it has its own fire-pit. That's where I carve, [by myself], whatever the weather."[16]

Another aspect of the typical working conditions of craft artists is related to potential hazards to their health. Many craft artists work with items that emit noxious fumes, like those from paint, ink, glue, spirit gum, liquid rubber, and other craft supplies. Dust, metal filings, or sawdust can also be present in the air; paint and cleaning fluids can sometimes spatter; and hot kilns and freshly blown glass can cause burns to exposed skin. It is therefore necessary for many craft artists to wear gloves, goggles, face masks, or other protective gear when working.

A Typical Workday for a Craft Artist

The way a workday goes for a craft artist very much depends on the type of artist, since each craft utilizes different materials and supplies. Also, different kinds of craft artists work at different speeds. An average project for a metalworker might take one or two weeks or more to complete, whereas a small vase made by a potter might be done in as little as a day.

Nevertheless, what all craft artists have in common is that they love and take pride in their work. Of course, they always hope that they can make a living doing that work. So a common goal among craft artists, and for that matter artists of all kinds, is to find a way to do the work they love and manage to get paid for it. That is, they hope to achieve the satisfaction that comes with being able to support themselves by expressing their innate creativity. Indeed, managing to achieve that goal is the biggest motivating factor in the average craft artist's life. In that regard, successful UK metalworking artist Anthony Tanner gives the following advice. Work hard and always "believe in yourself," he says. "Be patient and persevere, persevere, persevere, and if you have a day job don't rush to give it up. [In my own case] I became an 'overnight success' after 20 years of hard work, although I hope it doesn't take that long [for other creatives]."[17]

Find Out More
American Craft Council (ACC)

www.craftcouncil.org

The ACC supports craft artists of all kinds by helping organize public events that showcase their work and bring together artists from around the country. Its website contains information to aid young emerging artists and a searchable library of the history of American crafts.

American Quilters Society (AQS)

https://www.americanquilter.com

The AQS's goal is to provide a forum for quilters to excel at quilt making, artistic self-expression, and quilt collecting. The colorful website features a place to download *American Quilter* magazine, ways to obtain gift cards for quilting supplies, and tips and tutorials on various quilting techniques and ideas.

International Ceramic Arts Network (ICAN)

https://ceramicartsnetwork.org

ICAN is an online community that helps potters around the world, along with young people considering adopting this ancient, venerable craft. Its website contains numerous tips on ceramic techniques and "how-to" articles, including how to create an effective portfolio to showcase one's pottery.

CHAPTER THREE

Fine Artists

What Careers Do People Pursue in the Fine Arts?

Fine arts generally refers to artwork that is meant to be displayed—for example, in a gallery or museum—rather than having a specific function or use. The most common examples of fine artists who work in the visual arts are painters, sculptors, and stained glass artists. This type of artwork is usually meant to elicit some sort of emotional reaction (such as serenity, anger, confusion, or pleasure) in the viewer.

Fine arts can also include original music created by a composer. Composers create musical pieces that will be played later for audiences by musicians. But unlike those musicians, who are performing artists, composers do not usually perform those pieces. Rather, like other fine artists, composers create an artistic work from scratch. In this case the work consists of a large collection of notes and other printed symbols on paper, and when those notes are played by musicians, the sounds that are created elicit an emotional response in the listener. Indeed, the Bureau of Labor Statistics (BLS) explains that fine artists typically "create objects that are beautiful, thought provoking, and sometimes shocking. They often strive to communicate ideas or feelings through their art."[18]

Like craftspeople and other types of artists, fine artists display and, when possible, sell their works online or in art galleries, at town or county fairs, and at other venues. Although some fine artworks do end up in museums, most do not. Some paintings, statues, and other artworks, along with musical compositions, may be commissioned (requested and paid for by a client). But the bulk of fine artworks are created on spec (made at the artist's own time and expense). These artists typically spend a considerable amount of time trying to sell their work and build a reputation in the art or musical world.

Because acquiring such a reputation can be quite a difficult undertaking for most fine artists, many of their number hold down at least one other job to help support themselves. Not surprisingly, those artists who do take on side jobs desire to be around the creative endeavors they love. So it is not unusual for them to work in art galleries or on museum staffs or to teach various forms of art or music in local art institutes or schools.

How Do People Prepare for Careers in the Fine Arts?

Most fine artists get a formal education in the arts. Some aspiring artists obtain college or university degrees in a specific area of the arts. Others attend independent art institutes that grant fine arts certificates. Specific fields of study in the fine arts include painting, sculpture, and music.

In contrast, some fine artists are self-taught. This can be an uncertain and at times tortuous approach to producing art, but with enough perseverance it can lead to positive results. The great Mexican painter Frida Kahlo is a well-known example of a self-taught artist. In 1925, when she was eighteen, she was badly injured in a trolley accident that left her bedridden for many months. Years later, she recalled, "I never thought of painting until 1926, when I was in bed on account of [the accident]. I was bored as hell in bed with a plaster cast . . . so I decided to do something. I stole from my father some oil paints, and my mother ordered for me a special easel because I couldn't sit [up], and I started to paint."[19] At first, Kahlo practiced by creating self-portraits, and, learning a little from each attempt, she developed skills and a unique style that eventually brought her international fame.

In contrast to falling into the fine arts by accident, some young people seriously desire to enter them but are unable to do so

Artists Who Make a Living Teaching

For reasons that vary from person to person, some fine artists end up teaching their areas of expertise. In that regard, they can choose from diverse venues, including public schools, colleges and universities, art institutes, online websites, and private lessons. Those who choose the latter can charge $40, $50, or more per hour, especially in cities, where more residents can afford the luxury of art or music lessons. As for teaching in public schools, the BLS says that fine arts teachers in kindergarten to grade 12 average roughly $50,000 a year. (The exact amount varies from state to state.) That figure is closer to $70,000 for fine arts teachers at the college level. In comparison, teaching art or music courses online can be much more monetarily rewarding, given the right platform. If the teacher is well known in the art world, he or she can command fees adding up to several thousand dollars per month. One of the leading online fine arts teaching sites, Patreon, is essentially a portal through which thousands of artists based in dozens of countries offer classes and advice or otherwise connect with students, fans, or both.

because certain obstacles impede them. One such individual— self-taught Massachusetts-based composer Marvin Karp, now in his eighties, recalls:

> I wanted to formally study music when I was young, but various circumstances made that impossible. Still, I often daydreamed about becoming a composer because I could hear original music in my head. Much later in life, I started singing in local choral groups. That allowed me to learn some music structure and terminology. It wasn't long before I was able to start writing down some of the melodies floating inside my head. It was crude at first, but with desire, persistence, and eventually some superb advice from a wonderful composer friend, I was able to develop a smoother path for my musical ideas for various choral works, chamber works, and small-scale symphonic works.[20]

How Well Do Jobs in the Fine Arts Pay?

The pay that fine artists earn is extremely wide ranging, in part because there is no set pay scale in the fine arts. Also, the amount a fine artist earns often depends on factors such as level of experience and how well known the artist is. The work of a well-known artist is more likely to be in high demand—and thus lead to greater earnings—than the work of an unknown artist.

The nature of the art form can also affect what an artist earns. This frequently boils down to traditional marketing practices that are based on audience size—that is, what kinds of work sell to the most people. In the music world, for instance, a composer who writes a pop song that becomes a hit can make hundreds of thousands or even millions of dollars for a work that took only a few hours to create.

FACT

In 2021 the BLS listed annual income for the lowest-paid 10 percent of fine artists at about $22,000.

In comparison, an orchestral composer who is fortunate enough to have a symphonic work performed typically makes little or nothing for a project that took weeks or months to create. In such a case the composer's "pay" consists of the prestige gained from public exposure of the work. One exception is when a composer is expressly commissioned to create the work, in which case he or she makes a one-time fee of a few hundred or a few thousand dollars. Another exception is the case of successful film composers who produce orchestral music. They can command fees in the tens of thousands of dollars, or on occasion a few hundred thousand dollars. Thus, the earnings of fine artists can range from close to zero to millions of dollars, depending on diverse factors.

Most painters, sculptors, and other fine artists face this challenging situation regarding earnings. A small number of such artists, who have made a name for themselves, can make in excess of $100,000 per year. But the vast majority of visual artists make a fraction of that. In 2021 the BLS listed the annual salary for the lowest-paid 10 percent of such artists at about $22,000. But those were from the pool of fine artists who were working full time and trying to sell their art in public galleries, online, or elsewhere. The fact is that large numbers of creative people do such art part time and only rarely manage to sell any of their work. To the individuals in that group, successful oil painter Carrie L. Lewis gives this advice: "[You] *must* be prepared to build an audience and spend time and effort developing your business. For many [would-be] artists . . . this means the best plan is to work for someone else for a while . . . all the while building your art business on the side."[21]

Helpful Skills

Skills vary depending on the type of art. Successful painters, for example, should have a better than rudimentary ability to sketch people, animals, and objects. Even if an artist's chosen medium is not drawing, the ability to sketch helps him or her develop feelings for form, shadowing, perspective, and so forth. Painters also need to have a solid knowledge of the various artistic media and materials. The ability to manage time effectively, attention to detail, and fundamental computer skills are also basics for modern painters.

For music composers and arrangers, the ability to hear original music fully formed in one's head is vital. Composers need to be able to read music. They typically also play one or more musical instruments. Time management and attention to detail are no less crucial for composers than for painters and sculptors.

What Are the Working Conditions for Most Fine Artists?

Many fine artists work in private studios in their homes. Others do their work in studios located in warehouses, lofts, back rooms in art galleries, or rented spaces in office buildings. With rare exceptions, these individuals tend to work alone, preferring a degree of solitude that allows them to concentrate on the creative process.

The working conditions for some fine artists can be on the decidedly messy side. In particular, whether painters work in oils, acrylics, watercolors, or other media, they

FACT

With rare exceptions, most fine artists work alone, preferring a quiet environment that allows them to concentrate on the creative process.

Inspired by a Mentor

Many of the best-known fine artists were, as beginners in their fields, strongly influenced by experienced professionals who gave them valuable advice about how to develop their talents. For Lin-Manuel Miranda, who composed the music (and wrote the stage play) for the hit Broadway musical *Hamilton*, that influential mentor was the creator of stage musicals Stephen Sondheim (*West Side Story*, *A Little Night Music*, *Company*, *Sweeney Todd*). According to Miranda, who as a young man got to know Sondheim well:

> The biggest thing I take from Sondheim's writing is the element of surprise and variety. There's not one score where there isn't incredible rhythmic and melodic variety. When I was working on *Hamilton*, Steve really encouraged me to develop that piece, and I'd occasionally be brave enough to send him demos. Every time, he'd write back saying "variety, variety, variety." The tricky thing about writing hip hop for the stage is when our head starts bopping, we stop paying attention to the lyrics. It's important to always surprise the audience. I really took that feedback to heart.

Quoted in Freya Parr, "Lin-Manuel Miranda: 'Anyone Who Tells You That Sondheim Isn't an Influence on Their Music or Their Work Is Lying,'" Classical Music, January 14, 2022. www.classical-music.com.

almost always spill or drip multicolored globs on the floor, the easel, and any clothes they are wearing. That explains why most painters don expendable or disposable frocks or other clothing items before beginning to work.

A Typical Workday for a Fine Artist

With occasional exceptions, a majority of fine artists have a routine they develop and repeat daily until they finish a project. That routine is different for each artist. Some may work only mornings, for example; others may prefer afternoons or evenings. Similarly, some turn off their phones and otherwise eliminate possible interruptions, while others welcome occasional breaks to chat with family or friends.

Whatever kind of routine various artists maintain, most are always cognizant of their audience. All artists understand that they depend to some degree on the people who enjoy and buy their works. In the words of noted California painter David J. Rogers, an ever-present value of all art "is the emotional connection it has with the viewer. I'm always striving to make that connection in the purest and most honest way that I know of. My goal as an artist is always the same, that my work will hopefully provide a peaceful escape for the soul of the viewer."[22]

Find Out More

American Society of Composers, Authors and Publishers (ASCAP)

www.ascap.com

ASCAP is a professional organization of some 690,000 songwriters, composers, and music publishers, owned and run by its members. Its website lists job openings in the music industry and features a searchable database that tells who composed which songs and other musical pieces.

International Sculpture Center (ISC)

https://sculpture.org

Founded in 1960, the ISC works to promote a worldwide appreciation for the fine art of sculpture. Its handsomely mounted website has a section on openings for residencies (internships) in various countries; situations in which young sculptors can work with seasoned professionals.

Oil Painters of America (OPA)

https://www.oilpaintersofamerica.com

The OPA represents over thirty-five hundred artists throughout North America. Its main goals are to preserve and promote excellence in painting and to provide a forum in which artists can display their works. The website features advice on how to ship paintings and how painters can obtain scholarships and sponsors.

CHAPTER FOUR

Performing Artists

What Are the Careers That Performing Artists Pursue?

Several kinds of performing artists exist. Among the best known are actors, singers, dancers, musicians, stuntpersons, stand-up comics, and circus performers. Actors, along with chorus singers and dancers, most often work in stage shows, including Broadway shows, as well as in films and television. Dancers also appear in shows presented by well-known dance companies in diverse styles, among them ballet, traditional folk, and modern dance. And singers often pursue careers in no less varied styles, including opera, jazz, rock, hip-hop, and more.

There are a number of other kinds of performing artists as well. Among them are musicians who play in symphony orchestras, chamber groups, rock bands, folk groups, musical theater, and many other venues. Also, stuntpersons work mostly in film and television, while stand-up comics do both TV and live shows in theaters and nightclubs. In the meantime, although circus performers used to be confined to live tent shows that traveled from town to town, a major change came in the 1980s with the birth of Cirque du Soleil. In more than a dozen separate companies, its members perform in theaters, concert halls, sports stadiums, and television studios.

How Do People Prepare for Careers as Performing Artists?

In theory, the majority of performing artists do not need college degrees or other kinds of formal education to build a career.

If a person is extremely talented and happens to know the right people or is in the proverbial right place at the right time, he or she might become successful. However, although that scenario *has* happened now and then, it is *extremely* rare. Any would-be performer would benefit from getting as much training as possible in his or her chosen field.

A variety of options exist for obtaining education and training. Many young aspiring actors, for example, choose to enroll in college or university drama departments. Some of these colleges and universities have established strong reputations for their acting programs. Other aspiring actors seek out dedicated acting schools that have a long-standing tradition of giving beginning actors a place to hone their craft.

Widely seen as pivotal among these schools is the HB Studio, founded in 1945 by Broadway actor and director Herbert Berghof. In time, he and stage actress Uta Hagan, who began teaching there soon afterward, came to be seen as among the premier acting coaches of the twentieth century. Although they both died in 1990, the school they created endures with a new generation of distinguished teachers. A few of the hundreds of famous actors who attended the school over the years are Matthew Broderick, Barbra Streisand, Lily Tomlin, Claire Danes, and Al Pacino. Looking back, the incredibly successful Pacino says that his acting coach at the studio "introduced me to other worlds, to certain aspects of life I wouldn't have come in contact with. He introduced me to writers, the stuff that surrounds acting. For the first time, I knew I had something going for me, a chance to use myself, my life. [I came to] realize that acting is poetry, an art that employs the voice, the body, the spirit."[23]

Many aspiring dancers and musicians also benefit from formal training. Well-respected dance and music programs can be found at colleges and universities nationwide. Many private schools also offer lessons in dancing and playing various musical instruments. The schools with the most prestigious reputations tend to be in the bigger cities, particularly New York City,

Chicago, and Los Angeles. Dancers, singers, and musicians also have the alternative, if they can afford it, of taking private lessons from highly experienced performers who tutor beginners.

How Well Do Jobs in the Performing Arts Pay?

The amount of money that performing artists make varies a great deal, depending on several factors. These include how often they are able to find work, their level of experience, and whether they have a reputation that makes them in demand. According to the Bureau of Labor Statistics (BLS), the median pay of an actor (assuming she or he is not well known and therefore cannot command higher wages) is equivalent to about twenty-three dollars per hour.

FACT
According to the BLS, the median pay for actors amounts to about twenty-three dollars per hour.

Another factor that can affect the earnings of performing artists is whether they belong to a union, since union members automatically make a minimum base pay. Stage actors have the Actors' Equity Association (AEA); film actors and stuntpersons have the Screen Actors Guild (SAG); and the American Guild of Variety Artists (AGVA) represents dancers, singers, stand-up comics, circus performers, and other performing artists. In 2022 working AGVA and SAG members averaged about $52,000 per year, and AEA members averaged around $80,000 a year. More-experienced and better-known performers can and do earn a lot more—a few of them commanding salaries of hundreds of thousands or even millions of dollars per year.

Helpful Skills

In addition to a certain amount of basic talent, performing artists, no matter what their specialty might be, have a number of essential and desired skills and abilities in common. For example, actors, dancers, singers, stand-up comics, and musicians all require and seek to maintain a high level of confidence in themselves. It is a

Many Possible Job Venues for Actors

"Actors are employed in a range of settings," state the editors of the Britain-based Association of Graduate Careers Advisory Services.

> Repertory companies [regional professional theater groups] employ actors for a season, during which they perform in a number of different plays, each one usually running for a specified period. Commercial theatre companies produce plays or musicals, often for long runs in London's West End, [New York City's Broadway and Off-Broadway], or other locations, as well as tours. Fringe theatre companies are small companies, sometimes employing only a few staff and may specialise in a niche area of theatre or performance, or focus on work from a specific era or by a particular playwright. . . . Children's theatre companies . . . tour schools and other venues to entertain children. . . . Youth theatres engage with young people in theatre activities, outside the formal education system. Film, television and radio companies employ actors to work on particular productions. Contracts can range from a day to several months, or longer. Actors may also be employed to appear in promotional or training videos, or to participate in corporate training events, where they might facilitate role-play activities for staff.

Editors of the Association of Graduate Careers Advisory Services, "Job Profile: Actor," Prospects, May 1, 2021. www.prospects.ac.uk.

measure of self-assurance that makes it possible for them to perform in front of crowds of people without losing their composure. Related to that ability are two others that one needs to succeed as a performing artist—stamina and resilience. These translate into a strong capacity to absorb and respond well to criticism. The fact is that almost all performers endure at least some degree of rejection when breaking into their chosen professions, and they must be able to get past such rebuffs and keep on trying.

Performing artists also benefit from having as much personal flexibility as possible. According to Daniel Higginbotham, who runs a firm that helps talented college graduates find careers in creative fields, "Performers need to adapt and apply their skills and talent to a variety of roles, genres, techniques, and styles. For example, actors may be cast as a hero in one role and a villain in

the next, while dancers may be required to perform classical ballet for one job and street dance the week after."[24]

Some other skills that are helpful for performing artists vary according to the kind of performing that is involved. For example, those who stand and speak before a live audience—like actors and stand-up comics—need to have strong reading and memorization skills. They also require the ability to self-reflect and admit to themselves that a particular approach they are employing is not working and needs to be altered.

Meanwhile, particularly beneficial to musicians is having perfect pitch—the ability to identify any note in a scale simply by hearing it. And stuntpersons and circus performers are aided by attaining high levels of physical strength and endurance, since their jobs are extremely physical in nature.

What Are the Working Conditions for Performing Artists?

The majority of performing artists work within a very social atmosphere because they regularly interact with fellow artists, as well as audiences. Also, they tend to perform in large-scale venues, such as theaters, auditoriums, concert halls, film studios, and so forth. In addition, traveling from city to city or state to state is often involved, because actors, comics, singers, and circus acts often go on tour.

A Typical Workday for a Performing Artist

With rare exceptions, workdays for performing artists are long. Indeed, even if a performance by an actor, dancer, musician, comic, or circus clown lasts only two hours or so, several hours of preparation—often consisting of costuming, makeup, physical warm-ups, and run-throughs—are usually needed. Also, for weeks or sometimes months before performances of a show begin, the performers typically engage in long, grueling bouts of rehearsing. "While training," says Jennifer Rigby, a journalist who frequently writes about dancers,

> **FACT**
>
> Performing artists typically work long hours, with practices and rehearsals often lasing for weeks or months.

students will dance between six and seven hours a day. In most professional companies, a morning class at 10 starts the day, and they could rehearse through until 6pm, with breaks. This punishing schedule is usually done up to six days a week. On performance days, the class may begin slightly later, but then there will still be three or four hours of rehearsal before the three hour performance. Then the dancer will be back the next day to do it all again.[25]

Particularly taxing are the workdays of actors on film sets; while a movie or TV show is being shot, they typically work twelve-

How to Become a Circus Performer

Circus performer has long constituted one of the most specialized and exotic careers in the performing arts. The research team for the career-oriented company ZipRecruiter here describes that profession and how to enter it.

In this career, your job duties depend on which of the circus arts that you perform. Some examples of circus entertainment include trapeze artists, acrobats, daredevils, animal trainers, and circus clowns. There are also a number of supporting entertainment roles that can be available depending on the circus for which you work. There may be the need for dancers, artists, singers, and baton twirlers. This job requires extensive traveling. The qualifications needed for a career as a circus performer vary greatly depending on the type of performance that you plan to give. There are no universal educational requirements, but you should have significant training in your circus art. This training can be accomplished through self-teaching or by learning the skills as an apprentice with an experienced circus performer. You also need experience performing in front of large audiences. To actually land a circus performer job, you must audition to demonstrate your skills.

ZipRecruiter Marketplace Research Team, "What Is a Circus Performer and How to Become One." ZipRecruiter. www.ziprecruiter.com.

or even fourteen-hour days. In the words of film producer Gavin Polone, "It has always been difficult for me to understand how so many in this business put up with such a punishing routine."[26] The fact is that most actors do put up with it, in large part because they simply love the job. Actress Jennifer Beals says, "I like the day-to-day aspect of preparing and the physicality of it." No matter how long the hours may be, she explains, actors typically feel they "have to dive into every moment as fully as possible."[27]

Find Out More

American Guild of Variety Artists (AGVA)
https://agvausa.com
AGVA represents a wide variety of performing artists, including singers and dancers in touring shows, theme park performers,

skaters, circus performers, stand-up comics and comedians, cabaret and club artists. The organization's website features on-going news about the entertainment industry and tips about up-coming auditions.

International Stunt School
www.stuntschool.com
The International Stunt School is widely regarded as the most thorough and all-encompassing stunt training program in North America. Its colorful website describes the various kinds of stunts that members perform and lists the many recent movies in which members have appeared.

Screen Actors Guild–American Federation of Television and Radio Artists (SAG-AFTRA)
www.sagaftra.org
SAG-AFTRA strongly protects the rights of actors, dancers, sing-ers, stunt performers, and other kinds of performing artists. Its website section called MOVE (Members Organizing Volunteer Ef-forts) tells how members, young and old, can help expand the number of performing jobs available.

CHAPTER FIVE

Designers

What Are the Careers That Designers Pursue?

The many types of designers inhabiting the modern world of cultural creatives include fashion designers, costume designers, floral designers, jewelry designers, interior designers, and commercial and industrial designers, among others. Fashion designers create clothes, footwear, and accessories. Costume designers oversee the acquisition and making of costumes for stage shows, films, and television shows. In addition to standard clothing items, a stage costume often includes various accessories the actors wear or use while performing; for example, hats, gloves, shoes, canes, crowns, hair ribbons, war medals, gun holsters, tool belts, and masks. Designers also work with flowers and jewelry. Interior designers make indoor spaces like houses and offices attractive, functional, and safe. Finally, commercial and industrial designers create technical and manufactured products, including cars, home appliances, toys, and cell phones.

One thing that all of these designers have in common is that they create new products, or new versions of older products, that make life easier or more enjoyable—or both. According to the Bureau of Labor Statistics (BLS), "Designers make original creations that have practical or aesthetic purpose. Businesses in nearly all industries rely on designers to develop and implement ideas for products or services. Designers may start a project by sketching ideas on paper or creating a computer prototype. Feedback from clients and staff members helps refine the ideas into a final product."[28]

How Do People Prepare for Careers as Designers?

In regard to educational requirements for designers, much depends on the kind of design involved. For floral designers, for instance, the minimum requirement is a high school diploma in most cases. If a prospective floral designer wants to enhance his or her résumé with more education, in most states a few private floral schools, vocational schools, or community colleges offer individual classes. A person can also obtain experience by working in a local greenhouse or nursery.

In comparison, graphic designers, interior designers, costume designers, and fashion designers generally require a bachelor's degree. The National Association of Schools of Art and Design accredits over 360 colleges, universities, and independent institutes with majors or minors in one or all of these design categories. Many of the creative individuals who attend these schools know they want be designers from a fairly young age. A number of others, however, do not so early foresee themselves becoming designers. It is not unusual for those individuals to initially aim at other professions and later unexpectedly fall into the job of designer. This is what happened to the renowned fashion designer Donna Karan. She recalls that

> the last thing I wanted to do was [be a designer] on Seventh Avenue [in New York City]. . . . I thought [what] I would like to do is be an illustrator. I love drawing. I love drawing bodies. I love drawing fashion, but I wasn't thinking of myself as a designer in those days. And then I went for a job at *Women's Wear Daily* [magazine] and they said, you know, I think maybe you should look into design instead of illustration. . . . So I [sort of fell] into the fashion industry. I started working in Sherry's clothing store [in New York] when I was young and I love dressing people. . . . I liked working in [a] retail store, arranging it and making it look really pretty, making it easier for the customer. So I found that I was getting into fashion whether I liked it or not.[29]

How Well Do Designers' Jobs Pay?

Just as educational requirements for designers vary according to the type of design they practice, so does their pay. For example, according to the BLS, in 2021 floral designers' median pay was about $30,000 annually. Costume designers' median pay was roughly $40,000 to $45,000 that year, while graphic designers' median pay was $51,000. The median yearly salary of interior designers was $58,000 to $63,000, depending on their level of experience and the part of the country in which they worked. The best-paid designers in 2021 were those in the fashion industry, with a median yearly income of about $77,000.

FACT

In 2021 the median yearly income for fashion designers was about $77,000.

A key requirement for getting jobs in design and for receiving good, competitive pay for those jobs is having the best portfolio possible. As the BLS points out, "Developing a portfolio—a collection of design ideas that demonstrates their styles and abilities—is essential. [For example,] students studying fashion design often have opportunities to develop their portfolios further by entering their designs in student or amateur contests. When making hiring decisions, employers rely on these portfolios to gauge talent and creativity."[30]

Helpful Skills

Almost all designers, whatever their specialty may be, need an arsenal of specific skills and abilities. First and foremost, they should be highly creative, in the sense that they are able to boldly exercise their imaginations not just now and then, but on a consistent basis. Also essential is developing a unique style, or characteristic personal approach to designing, which sets one apart from others in the business. All designers should also be detail oriented, have a good sense of proportion and color coordination, and demonstrate strong communication skills. The latter is

A Costume Designer Describes Her Profession

Deborah Nadoolman Landis works as a costume designer and also runs the David C. Copley Center for the Study of Costume Design in Los Angeles. She explains the essence of the job of a costume designer.

> Every garment worn in a movie is considered a costume. Costumes are one of many tools the director has to tell the story. Costumes communicate the details of a character's personality to the audience, and help actors transform into new and believable people on screen. There is often confusion between costume design and fashion design; however, these two fields and their objectives are very different. Fashion designers have labels and sell their clothes, while costume designers have no labels and are focused on creating authentic characters in a story. Costume designers create both beautiful gowns for a glamorous entrance and everyday clothes when required by the script. They must know "who" characters "are" before they create a closet of clothes and accessories for the characters. A costume is worn by one actor, as one specific character, in a specific scene or scenes in the story. Most important, the audience must believe that every person in a story has a life before the movie begins.

Deborah Nadoolman Landis, "Costume Design: Defining Character," Academy of Motion Picture Arts and Sciences, 2014. www.oscars.org.

imperative, both for dealing with clients and selling oneself to prospective employers and the general public.

What Are the Typical Working Conditions for Designers?

Most designers work in offices, workrooms in the back areas of shops, and small factories. And some work at least part of each week at home and use email and Zoom to communicate with bosses, fellow designers, assistants, or clients. In general, design jobs tend to be fairly social in nature because of the number of people designers are in contact with in a typical week. Canadian costume designer Judith Bowden, for instance, says that she works "closely with the other designers (lighting, set, etc.) and also with the actors who will be wearing the final result."[31]

Another aspect of working conditions that is similar for all kinds of designers is the need for up-to-date technology. Today almost all design work is done with a combination of initial sketches done by hand and finalized designs fashioned with the aid of specialized computer software. Thus, at least some cutting-edge computer equipment is essential no matter where a designer is based.

In a different vein, working hours for designers often vary according to factors such as where the person is located and the nature of the area of design he or she practices. Floral designers in small or medium-sized towns, for example, may work regular nine-to-five hours most of the time and need to put in overtime only on holidays traditionally associated with giving flowers, such as Valentine's Day, Easter, and Mother's Day. In contrast, a floral designer in a busy shop in a large city may be required to work long hours on a regular basis simply because the customer base is larger.

The nature of costume, interior, and graphic designing is often different. It is common in those professions, for instance, to

A woman participates in a Zoom call with a client. Some designers work part of each week at home and use email and Zoom to communicate with bosses, fellow designers, assistants, or clients.

be busy and put in long hours primarily when working on commissioned projects, each of which might last a few weeks or months. When the job is done, there may or may not be a slower period before the

next project begins. Of course, large and prestigious design firms or well-known individual designers are typically in high demand and therefore may be quite busy all year long.

A Typical Workday for a Designer

It is nearly impossible to describe a typical day for designers in general, in part because there are many different kinds of designers. Also, even within a specific design area, individual designers follow markedly different schedules. Some work in offices, while others work mainly at home. New York City–based graphic designer Hayden Davis, who works mostly from home, describes his typical workday:

> [Each morning] I get on my phone as I gradually get up, moving to my desk where I put on some music, check emails, make checklists, and work on projects. I often start working before getting ready for the day, so showering and getting changed ends up getting postponed until the moment before I go out [to dinner]. . . . I am a complete night owl. I seem to be the most motivated and productive at 11:00 pm. . . . When 2:00 am rolls around I remember I was supposed to go to bed hours before. Luckily, my schedule lets me work as late as I want/need.[32]

In contrast, other kinds of designers spend much less time at home and much more time in offices and other outside locations. According to the BLS, for example, "Graphic designers generally work in studios, where they have access to equipment such as drafting tables, computers, and software. Although many graphic

What Graphics Designers Do

There are many different kinds of designers. The Bureau of Labor Statistics here differentiates graphic designers from the others.

Graphic designers, also referred to as graphic artists or communication designers, combine art and technology to communicate ideas through images and the layout of websites and printed pages. They may use a variety of design elements to achieve artistic or decorative effects. Graphic designers work with both text and images. They often select the type, font, size, color, and line length of headlines, headings, and text. Graphic designers also decide how images and text will go together in print or on a webpage, including how much space each will have. When using text in layouts, graphic designers collaborate with writers, who choose the words and decide whether the words will be put into paragraphs, lists, or tables. Through the use of images, text, and color, graphic designers may transform data into visual graphics and diagrams to make complex ideas more accessible. Graphic design is important to market and sell products, and it is a critical component of brochures and logos. Therefore, graphic designers often work closely with people in advertising and promotions, public relations, and marketing.

Bureau of Labor Statistics, "What Graphic Designers Do," September 8, 2022. www.bls.gov.

designers work independently, those who work for specialized graphic design firms are often part of [an office-based] design team."[33] It is recommended, therefore, that anyone who wants to become a designer first look into the typical working environment within the design area he or she seeks to enter.

Find Out More
American Society of Interior Designers (ASID)
www.asid.org
The ASID promotes the values and contributions of interior design in society. The society's website features helpful sections on how to find commercial sponsors, yearly awards won by members, and an annual competition for the best portfolios by beginning designers.

Costume Designers Guild (CDG)

https://costumedesignersguild.com

The CDG works to raise the stature of costume designers in the entertainment industry. The guild's beautifully mounted website has a section on educational opportunities for aspiring costume designers, plus color pictures of iconic costumes from many well-known films.

Council of Fashion Designers of America (CFDA)

https://cfda.com

The CFDA, established in 1962, has almost five hundred members, who design most of America's finest women's wear, menswear, jewelry, and clothing accessories. Its website contains a section explaining how would-be fashion designers can get training and scholarships.

CHAPTER SIX

Media and Communications Artists

What Are the Careers That Media and Communications Artists Pursue?

Media and communications artists, often shortened to simply "media artists," are creative individuals who specialize in conveying information from one party or group to another. Overall, media artists keep the general public up-to-date about news; social, political, and scientific trends and developments; and other relevant information. The most familiar kinds of media artists include journalists, book and magazine editors, photographers, cartoonists, illustrators, digital artists, technical writers, internet-based writers, and general writers of fiction and nonfiction.

Of these professions, probably the best known to the general public are writers of fiction and nonfiction books and articles. According to Zippia, an online site that provides detailed information about careers of all kinds, in 2022 close to 1 million books were published in the United States alone. That equates to over 2,500 books per day, or put another way, more than 100 books per hour. And that counts only those books put out by publishers. Another approximately 3 million books were self-published by their writers.

Besides such writers, editors of books and articles are perhaps the most numerous media artists. According to the Bureau of Labor Statistics (BLS), editors "plan, review, and revise written material for publication. They coordinate with writers to explore ideas, establish a schedule, and maintain style standards. When reviewing and revising drafts, editors try to preserve the author's voice while verifying facts, correcting grammar, and reorganizing content to improve readability."[34]

Also numerous and well known to the public are journalists who investigate and report news stories in print, on TV, and in other media and writers who create articles, blogs, and other kinds of text for the internet. Less well known to most people, but no less active in the media and society, are technical writers. Some write how-to guides. Others write manuals that provide operating instructions for equipment and online devices and programs. According to Josh Fechter, founder of the online site Technical Writer HQ, "Technical writing is the art and science of communicating complex information to a non-technical audience."[35]

How Do People Prepare for Careers as Media and Communications Artists?

Media artists typically communicate language and ideas to wide audiences. And the most successful ones are usually those who are the most skillful at conveying information. Not surprisingly, therefore, employers generally expect them to be well educated. As a result, the majority of aspiring media artists need to obtain at least a bachelor's degree. More often than not, they major in subjects like English, creative writing, communications, or journalism.

Some sort of prior experience in the field one wants to enter is also helpful when searching for employment in most forms of media art. As the BLS points out, writers often gain such experience by working for high school and college newspapers, for local or regional magazines, at local radio and television stations, or in entry-level positions in advertising and publishing firms. In addition, numerous newspapers and magazines across the country offer internships for students, who typically do research, conduct interviews, and so forth. In today's increasingly technologically

Education Through Reading

Besides getting a well-rounded education—preferably with at least a bachelor's degree—to prepare to be a writer of fiction and nonfiction for young people, one should do as much reading as possible. This is the advice of Matt Ralphs, a successful author of books for children and young adults. "Writers learn from reading," he explains.

> When writers read, they can decide what works, what doesn't; what they love; what they hate; what makes them go "meh." The more you read, the more techniques and skills you'll assimilate. Your brain will soak it all up, without your even realizing. A writer should read widely. Books of all genres: adult, children's, romance, adventure, horror, literary fiction, Westerns, sci-fi, fantasy, classics. And not only novels. They should read newspapers too, and magazines, and poems, and short stories, and film scripts. Anything written can teach something, even if it's what NOT to do.

Quoted in Ol James, "Is It Hard to be a Children's Author? Expert Interview," Letter Review, April 21, 2022. https://letterreview.com.

based society, all prospective media artists should have at least basic computer skills, and those who possess advanced digital skills have a definite edge over those who do not.

Preparation for the profession of editor is similar in many ways to that for writers. As the BLS states:

> Editors typically need a bachelor's degree in English or a related field, such as communications or journalism. Candidates with other backgrounds who can show strong writing skills also may find jobs as editors. Editors who deal with specific subject matter may need related work experience. For example, fashion editors may need expertise in fashion that they gain through formal training or work experience.[36]

As for photographers, those who do portrait photography typically do not require college degrees. However, those who want to work in journalism (photojournalists), communications, or scientific disciplines more often than not need a bachelor's degree.

In contrast, many media artists who create articles and blogs for the internet have only a high school diploma. Most who are in that situation tend to gain experience and expertise over time by continuing to produce online content.

How Well Do Media and Communications Artists' Jobs Pay?

The pay for media artists can vary considerably, according to the kind of work done, experience level, education, and other factors. This wide range of possible earnings—from very little to a great deal—can be seen in the case of writers. Many people assume that for a writer to publish one or more books is almost always a very lucrative venture. But the reality can be quite different. In fact, most writers are far from rich, says successful children's author Matt Ralphs: "There are a few extremely successful authors, whose books sell by the pallet-load, and are made into films and TV shows and so on. But they're the exception. There are some writers who make enough money to live on, and many more who don't. Most writers I know have second jobs or supplementary incomes to bridge the financial gap not filled by book sales."[37]

Indeed, of the several hundred thousand writers in the United States who try to make a living at writing, most end up in one of two groups. Either they never manage to get paid for their writings, or they make a minimal amount from one or a few low-paying writing assignments and must work a second job to make ends meet. Meanwhile, on the other end of the pay range are the five best-selling authors in the world. For the period from June 2018 to June 2019, that group included J.K. Rowling, James Patterson, Michelle Obama, Jeff Kinney, and Stephen King. According to *Forbes*, these authors made a combined income of $235 million for that twelve-month period. With this vast gap between the ends of the pay scale, it is close to impossible

FACT

According to *Forbes* magazine, the world's five most successful writers made a combined income of $235 million during the twelve-month period between 2018 and 2019.

to denote an average salary for people who call themselves writers.

Therefore, estimates for writers' annual earnings by the BLS, Zippia, and other employment experts are based on those writers who are more or less steadily employed in one form or another through most of each year. The BLS estimates that about 140,000 of them exist in the United States, including freelance writers, medical writers, sportswriters, technical writers, speechwriters, writers for libraries and schools, science writers, ghostwriters, copywriters, and others. In 2022, Zippia says, the lowest paid averaged around $40,000 and the highest paid made about $107,000. In comparison, that same year editors averaged about $52,000 and journalists and photojournalists roughly $60,000.

Helpful Skills

Writers, editors, and other media artists need to be not only creative and adept at language but also very adaptable and reliable. In part this is because they often have to meet various deadlines and adapt to the rules of a given publisher or to the styles of new writers or editors they have never dealt with before. They also need to have up-to-date computer skills and familiarity with software that is commonly used by writers and editors. Critical-thinking skills are also helpful, as is the ability to do extensive research both quickly and accurately.

What Are the Typical Working Conditions for Media and Communications Artists?

Some media artists, such as writers, tend to work in relative solitude, often in their homes, although most of them can in theory work anywhere as long as they have access to a computer and email. By contrast, most journalists tend to work around other people, including fellow journalists and the people they interview or investigate.

Regarding hours, some writers and other media artists work part time. Others work full time and set their own hours on a daily or weekly basis. Still others prefer to maintain regular office hours for one reason or another, one motivation being that it allows them to keep up a traditional routine.

A Typical Workday for a Media and Communications Artist

Although there is no typical workday for all, or even most, media artists, many in that group of professions will recognize familiar elements within the following sample workday described by technical writer Phil Davis:

> I start early (5am) to catch our offices in NYC and London. . . . I work through emails, Slack, and Twitter to warm up my brain and to groom my to-do list for the day. . . . Then I work through my to-do list: writing docs, distributing drafts for review, posting final docs, pinging folks via email and face-to-face with questions about priorities, scheduling, and the content itself.[38]

Similarly, many editors will feel they have much in common with Katie Cline, a book editor for Atlantic Publishing in Ocala, Florida, who says,

> My day-to-day life as an editor is super hectic and sometimes frustrating, but I'm blessed to come to work every day and do what I'm passionate about. An author does the all-important work of creating a raw [piece of writing]. An editor just polishes the rough edges and makes it shine. Every chapter I rearrange, every phrase I manipulate, and every comma I shift takes a book one step closer to finding its way into the hands of a reader who will carry the book's information with them forever.[39]

A Book Editor Describes Her Job

Katie Cline, a book editor for Atlantic Publishing in Ocala, Florida, talks about the duties she performs on a regular basis.

First of all, nothing is ever done in red pen anymore. [Instead] everything is edited in Microsoft Word using the Track Changes function (which admittedly often shows changes in a red font). I don't sit in a high-rise office in New York City with interns bringing me Starbucks and steaks . . . but rather in a cubicle surrounded by sticky-notes in Florida. And most importantly, my day is anything but tranquil. At any one time, I might have anywhere from three to four authors' manuscripts in various stages of editing. . . . One manuscript might be fresh from the author after just signing the contract, and another might be in the very final stages before heading to design. . . . On top of all of this, I talk directly with authors via email and phone to understand their vision. I coordinate with the project manager who oversees the process to do things like write or edit book copy and ensure that the designer's cover design matches the tone of the manuscript.

Katie Cline. "A Day in the Life of an Editor," Atlantic Publishing Group, Inc., July 25, 2018. https://atlanticpublishing.wordpress.com.

No matter what their workdays may be like, media artists do jobs that help keep the wheels of society turning. According to Mary A. White of the Columbia University Teachers College in New York City, as the media have come to occupy a central place in our lives, society needs the most effective media experts possible to keep the populace informed. "Information is shifting from print to imagery," she points out, "and the shift [is] affecting deeply how we see our world, how we think about it, and how we solve its problems."[40]

Find Out More

American Society of Journalists and Authors (ASJA)

www.asja.org

The ASJA helps journalists and independent nonfiction writers navigate the fast-changing world of writing within the communications industry. Its website tells how to obtain the *ASJA Magazine* and information on how to go about finding potential publishers and agents.

American Society of Media Photographers (ASMP)

www.asmp.org

The ASMP is dedicated to protecting the rights and creative works of photographers who work in various positions in the media. Its extensive website has information about job openings, courses that beginners can take, and ways to ask questions of experienced professionals.

Writers Guild of America West (WGAW)

www.wga.org

Founded in 1933, the WGAW is a union that represents writers of film and TV scripts, broadcast news programs, and other forms of written content. Its user-friendly website features a section that tells how to register a script, a list of job openings, and a list of agents who represent writers.

Introduction: Showing the World One's True Self

1. Sergey Faldin, "How to Win at the Game of Life as a Struggling Artist," Writing Cooperative, December 26, 2019. https://writing cooperative.com.

2. Quoted in Arleen Kinsella, "A New Study Shows That Most Artists Make Very Little Money, with Women Faring the Worst," Artnet, November 29, 2017. https://news.artnet.com.

3. Tim Rettig, "How Long Does It Take to Make a Living from Your Art?," Art Plus Marketing, June 21, 2018. https://artplusmarket ing.com.

4. Quoted in Afzal Ibrahim, "What Is Art? Why Is It Important?," The Artist. www.theartist.me/art/what-is-art.

5. Quoted in Susan Gabriel, "Virginia Woolf Memoir: A Sketch of the Past," Susan Gabriel (personal website), July 29, 2010. www.susangabriel.com.

6. Quoted in Denis Vilorio, "Careers for Creative People," Bureau of Labor Statistics, June 1, 2015. www.bls.gov.

7. David J. Rogers, "The Artist," David J. Rogers Watercolor Artist, 2023. www.davidjrogersart.com.

8. Faldin, "How to Win at the Game of Life as a Struggling Artist."

Chapter One: Art Directors

9. Quoted in Creative Bloq Staff, "Being an Art Director: All You Need to Know," Creative Bloq, May 30, 2019. www.creative bloq.com.

10. Bureau of Labor Statistics, "How to Become an Art Director," September 8, 2022. www.bls.gov.

11. Quoted in Job Shadow, "Interview with an Art Director," 2023. https://jobshadow.com.

12. Quoted in Job Shadow, "Interview with an Art Director."

13. Quoted in Creative Bloq Staff, "Being an Art Director."

Chapter Two: Craft Artists

14. Andrew Jones, phone and email interview with the author, November 25, 2022.

15. Jones, interview.

16. Quoted in Great British Life, "The Art of Whittling Sticks in West Lancashire," December 11, 2017. www.greatbritishlife.co.uk.
17. Quoted in Smart Artist Hub, "Life Experience, Metalwork & Buddhas: An Interview with Anthony Tanner," 2022. www.smartartisthub.com.

Chapter Three: Fine Artists
18. Bureau of Labor Statistics, "What Craft and Fine Artists Do," September 8, 2022. www.bls.gov.
19. Quoted in Bertram D. Wolfe. "Rise of Another Rivera," *Vogue*, November 1, 1938, p. 131.
20. Marvin Karp, interview with the author, November 20, 2022.
21. Carrie L. Lewis, "How Much Money Do Artists Make in a Year?," EmptyEasel. https://emptyeasel.com.
22. Rogers, "The Artist."

Chapter Four: Performing Artists
23. Quoted in Delancyplace, "Al Pacino Was Homeless," August 17, 2017. https://delanceyplace.com.
24. Daniel Higginbotham, "7 Skills You Need to Succeed in Performing Arts," Prospects, April 1, 2022. www.prospects.ac.uk.
25. Jennifer Rigby, "How Hard Is the Life of a Professional Ballet Dancer?," Channel 4 News, January 25, 2012. www.channel4.com.
26. Quoted in V. Renée, "Are Film and TV Set Hours Still Brutal?," No Film School, October 23, 2019. https://nofilmschool.com.
27. Quoted in Cameron Stuart, "9 Actors Talk How Many Hours They Actually Spend on Set," *Backstage*, September 27, 2019. www.backstage.com.

Chapter Five: Designers
28. Bureau of Labor Statistics, "Careers for Creative People," June 1, 2015. www.bls.gov.
29. Quoted in Terry Gross, "Donna Karan on Motherhood, Fashion and Designing the Perfect Pair of Jeans," *Fresh Air*, NPR, October 12, 2015. www.npr.org.
30. Bureau of Labor Statistics, "How to Become a Fashion Designer," September 8, 2021. www.bls.gov.
31. Quoted in Retold Theatre, "Show Day and the Final Result," May 21, 2013. https://retoldtheatre.blogs.lincoln.ac.uk.
32. Quoted in Renee Fleck, "5 Freelance Graphic Designers Share Their Daily Routines," Dribble, September 22, 2021. https://dribble.com.

33. Bureau of Labor Statistics, "Graphic Designers," September 8, 2022. www.bls.gov.

Chapter Six: Media and Communications Artists
34. Bureau of Labor Statistics, "Careers for Creative People."
35. Josh Fechter, "Technical Writer Job Description Examples: Roles and Responsibilities," Technical Writer HQ, 2023. https://technical writerhq.com.
36. Bureau of Labor Statistics, "How to Become an Editor," September 8, 2022. www.bls.gov.
37. Quoted in Ol James, "Is It Hard to Be a Children's Author? Expert Interview," Letter Review, April 21, 2022 https://letterreview.com.
38. Quoted in Jacklyn, "A Typical Day for a Technical Writer," Medium, March 2, 2019. https://medium.com.
39. Katie Cline. "A Day in the Life of an Editor," Atlantic Publishing Group, Inc., July 25, 2018. https://atlanticpublishing.wordpress.com.
40. Quoted in Minnesota Governor's Council, "Media Arts," April 5, 2020. https://mn.gov.

Andrew Jones is the owner of and chief ceramic artist for the popular Earth-n-Fire Pottery shop in East Sandwich, on historic Cape Cod in Massachusetts. He specializes in custom-made stoneware and porcelain pottery, both functional and decorative, including lamps, bowls, teapots, platters, and serving pieces. Also, his unique creation—the Cape Cod Sea Gull—is well known throughout Massachusetts. Jones answered questions about his work via phone and email.

Q: Why and how did you become a potter?

A: From a young age I loved drawing, painting, sculpture, movies, music—anything to do with the arts. Fortunately, where I live there is an educational system and community dedicated to the arts and crafts. In addition, there is a thriving local crafts-based economy, along with positive examples of successful people in almost every artistic medium. All of this inspired me to pursue a life in the arts. After working preliminarily in a variety of artistic disciplines, I discovered clay and the potter's wheel. I started out by taking classes and then got involved with local potters, most often volunteering my time in exchange for lessons. In cases like that I did a lot of odd jobs, like mixing clay and sweeping the place and emptying the trash, but it was worth it because sometimes the potter would take me aside and show me how to do key tasks in the ceramic process. Eventually I eagerly acquired my own kiln and wheel and began consistently producing pottery ware. I found that firing the kiln routinely and repeatedly accelerates the learning curve and in time my skills at the wheel improved as well. Eventually I found full-time employment at a pottery shop and also threw [fashioned] pots for another studio potter. When I reached a level of sufficient confidence, I opened my own shop—a home-based studio gallery.

Q: Can you describe your typical workday?

A: A typical day for me consists of producing ware, finishing [glazing or painting] it, and of course marketing it. Most potters have multiple projects in production, each in a different stage of development. One learns early on that clay demands a lot of attention. Indeed, once a project is started, you have to follow through to completion or else risk losing the piece. Therefore, careful planning is always essential. Each piece will require considerable attention to detail. One has to try hard to find a balance between form and function, color, style, and customers' demands, all the time pursuing economy and efficiency. The best way to ensure a successful firing is to understand the material and have some control over the process. Firing pottery in kilns is an often difficult and tricky process. Once you've started, you have to achieve the appropriate temperature to achieve positive results. . . . It can take up to two weeks of effort to produce only a few small items. So *patience* is the number one quality needed by a potter to accomplish consistently desired outcomes. Working in stages or cycles is the common practice for making both functional ware and more artistically designed ware. Each potter/artist has to figure out how to improvise and adapt to a given work space; meet customer demand on a regular basis; do consistently good work; and hopefully manage to evolve as a creative person.

Q: What do you like most and least about your job?

A: The thing I like most about my job is that I have had the opportunity to create a way of life, or workable space, within the arts, which I love so much. I am also happy that being a potter has given me a strong feeling of independence as a person. As for what I like the least about the job is that when one does what he loves, there is usually not enough time in a typical day to do everything he wants to do! Therefore, potters and other craft artists need to know when, now and then, to take a much-needed break!

Q: What personal qualities do you find most valuable for this type of work?

A: Because you can't force clay to do what it simply cannot do, a potter needs to be patient, adaptable, and disciplined. It also helps to be your own worst critic and have a thick skin because, as in all the arts, there are plenty of would-be critics out there waiting to tell you what they don't like about your work.

Q: What advice do you have for students who might be interested in this career?

A: If you want to be an effective potter, and in general a successful artist, it helps to start by striving to be a good person in the first place. People will eventually notice your passion for your craft and your dedication and high level of commitment. Also, try, if at all possible, to pursue every promising opportunity that may come along.

Actor
Animator
Architect
Art gallery director
Biographer
Book illustrator
Camera operator
Choreographer
Cinematographer
Circus performer
Costume designer
Dancer
Documentary film maker
Doll maker
Fiction writer
Film director
Film editor
Floral designer
Foley artist for film and TV
Historian
Interior decorator
Jewelry designer
Magician
Makeup artist
Matte painter for film and TV
Metalworker
Museum curator

Musical composer
Music arranger
Music editor
Musician
Nonfiction writer
Orchestral conductor
Painter
Photographer
Playwright
Potter (ceramic artist)
Screenwriter
Sculptor
Set decorator
Singer
Special effects designer
Special effects supervisor
Stained glass window
   designer
Stand-up comedian
Stuntperson for film and TV
Storyboard artist
Tattoo artist
Toy designer
Video game designer
Voiceover artist
Web designer
Woodworker

Editor's note: The online *Occupational Outlook Handbook* of the US Department of Labor's Bureau of Labor Statistics is an excellent source of information on jobs in hundreds of career fields, including many of those listed here. The *Occupational Outlook Handbook* may be accessed online at www.bls.gov/ooh.

INDEX

PICTURE CREDITS

ABOUT THE AUTHOR

In addition to turning out numerous acclaimed volumes on ancient civilizations, as well as medieval and American history, historian Don Nardo has an extensive background in the creative arts, having worked as an actor with the National Shakespeare Company, among other theatrical groups; a makeup artist; a screenwriter with work for Warner Brothers and ABC TV; and a composer and arranger of orchestral music, with a number of commissions from symphony orchestras and musicians. He lives with his wife, Christine, in Massachusetts.